Little Things
Long Remembered

· ♡ ·

Other Books by Susan Newman

Parenting an Only Child
The Joys and Challenges of Raising
Your One and Only

Never Say Yes to a Stranger
What Your Child Must Know to Stay Safe

You Can Say No to a Drink or a Drug
What Every Kid Should Know

It Won't Happen to Me
True Stories of Teen Alcohol and Drug Abuse

Don't Be S. A. D.
A Teenage Guide to Stress, Anxiety and Depression

Little Things Long Remembered

Making Your Children Feel Special Every Day

Susan Newman, Ph.D.

Illustrated by Jennifer Harper

Crown Publishers, Inc.
New York

Published by Crown Publishers, Inc., 201 East 50th Street, New York New York 10022. Member of the Crown Publishing Group.

Random House, Inc. New York, Toronto, London, Sydney, Auckland

http://www.randomhouse.com/

CROWN is a trademark of Crown Publishers, Inc.

Printed in the United States of America

Library of Congress Cataloging-in-Publication Data
Newman, Susan
  Little things long remembered: making your children feel special
  every day
  p.   cm.
  1. Parenting—Miscellanea. 2. Child rearing—Miscellanea.
I. Title.
HQ755.8.N53   1993
649'.1—dc20   92-42897
                                                             CIP

ISBN 0-517-59302-5

15 14

For Andrew,
my constant inspiration.

· ♡ ·

And with special thanks to Janet Spencer King,
Irene Prokop, and Connie Lustig.

Contents

· ♡ ·

Little Things
Long Remembered

· ♡ ·

Connecting

Feeling overcommitted and overextended? Finding it a challenge to keep up with your own *and* your children's conflicting activities? If you sometimes feel you're out of touch with your children or are missing entirely too much of their childhood, *Little Things Long Remembered* can help.

This small book is a collection of ideas and reminders to bring you and your children closer while making efficient use of your available and generally limited time. Consider it your think tank for ways to stay involved in their lives no matter how busy you are. In spite of a totally impossible schedule, you'll be amazed at how many "connections" you can make with a child in a single day.

Children's reactions are unpredictable. You never know which gesture, tradition, or offbeat, spur-of-the-moment adventure will become a "little thing long remembered"—embedded happily and fondly in their minds forever.

The Cardinal Rules

· ♡ ·

Don't take your children for granted. When there's no time to talk, deliver a hug, a kiss, and a quick "I Love You."

Keep promises. Broken promises break down even the strongest parent/child bonds.

Limit social engagements. It's impossible to remain close to children if you have no time to be with them.

Don't let too much time pass between "little things." Make one a day your absolute minimum.

Clear your head of office problems and unwind before you arrive home. Reserve home time for focusing as much as possible on the children.

Don't decrease discipline because you feel guilty about the time you are away from home.

Take a half an hour or so for yourself now and then so that you have the energy to enjoy your children.

Choose activities you like because children can tell when you are not having fun.

And remember, the most precious time is the time you spend with your children.

Establishing Ties

When the rat race takes over, it's easy to forget the obvious. Here, attitudes, gestures, and techniques in abundance help you connect with your offspring and maintain those connections. Some are familiar, but forgotten, others will be new to your family. Pick and choose to match your needs, your children's ages, and everyone's disposition. Many are designed to make *you* as happy as your children.

A Special Place

Keep an extra chair or stool in the kitchen, den, next to your dressing table, in your home office or workshop area so your child can be with you easily to watch or talk.

House Rule I

Be sure you always give and receive hello and good-bye kisses from your children. If you don't get them, ask.

House Rule II

If there's been a misunderstanding or disagreement, straighten it out before bedtime.

Early Start

Kiss your child good-bye even if he's asleep when you leave for work.

Hi, Kids, I'm Home

Whenever you arrive home from work, try to be cheerful and happy to see your children no matter how tired you may be.

Role Model

Explaining how you spent *your* day encourages a child to open up and pour out the details of her day.

Designer Kiss

Develop a kiss that is unique to your family—its "trademark." Two pecks on the tip of the nose; one peck on each cheek; one long, two short kisses on the forehead.

"I Wanna Hold Your Hand"

The Beatles had the right idea. Whatever happened to hand-holding? Bring it back long after you would routinely hold your child's hand as a safety precaution.

> *Note: At different stages, children balk at public affection. Respect their wishes.*

Silent Communication

Thumbs up, hands out to the sides, quiet clapping, the peace sign, a wink, or gentle tug on an earlobe—invent a silent symbol of your family's camaraderie.

Compliments

Compliment your child *and* let your child overhear you complimenting him to someone else.

It's My Mom's

Lend your daughter a piece of your costume jewelry to wear to school or on the weekend.

What's Mine Is Yours

Dive into a hot-fudge sundae together. Share an apple or a banana. Split a piece of pie for dessert.

It's My Dad's
Lend your daughter a tie to wear as a belt. Lend your son a tie to wear as a tie.

I Chose You
Tell your child how much you enjoy being his parent. Children like to hear that they are loved and fun to be with.

Bravo
Let your child know that you are happy with her successes be they great or modest. Don't compare her with friends.

Important Hugs
One-on-one hugs tell a child he is special. When you embrace your child, give him and the hug your full attention.

Believer
For as long as your child believes, be the tooth fairy.

Sorry
Admit when you're wrong.

How's Jamie?
Inquire about your children's friends regularly.

Pet Names

As your child gets older, don't drop pet names—Pumpkin, Dumpling, Funny Face—just select them carefully to avoid embarrassment.

Mom, Come Look

If it's important enough for your child to ask you to see something she has done, it's important enough for you to take a look . . . and smile.

Praise Freely

By praising jobs well done and saying thank you for tasks completed you let your child know you recognize his efforts.

Not Now

Children are not responsible for your working too many hours. Don't use "I'm too tired" as an excuse too often.

Clearing the Air

When you're upset by something that happened at the office and ranting and raving at home, let your child know that you are not angry with her. Considering your child's feelings helps bridge the gap between office and home emotions.

Listen

"You're not listening," is generally a parent's cry to a child. To understand what is going on in your child's life, stop what you are doing, turn around, and pay attention to what she is saying.

Stop Nagging

Limit your demands to a predetermined number per day. Count and stop when you've used up your allotment.

I Want It, Too

Consult your child when it's time to buy birthday gifts for his friends. You'll find out what your child likes when he tells you what he thinks is a good present for a friend.

Leave On the Light

What seems silly to adults matters to children. Respect their wishes to leave on the hall light or not to tell someone something they feel is embarrassing.

Kissing Monster

If your style includes open affection, call yourself the "kissing monster" and plant kisses on your child in rapid profusion. Laughter will abound.

You Can Always Reach Me

Whether you are going to work or to visit friends, show your child where you have written the telephone number and give her permission to call you.

Note: If your home phone has memory, program in your office number so that a very young child has only one digit to remember.

That's Great!

Get excited when your child tells you about his day or his latest accomplishment. Nodding your head is not enough.

How Pretty

Wear whatever "jewels" your child makes or buys for you.

Quick Peek

Slip a picture of yourself or the family into your child's pocket or backpack.

Food, Glorious Food

Yes, the way to a child's heart is often through her stomach. Pick out one of her favorite snacks when you are zipping down the supermarket aisles.

Dinner Bell

Have a "chain call" to bring everyone to the table: Pam calls Lisa, Lisa calls Beth, Beth calls Pete. Or ring a bell to call the family together.

Study Hall

Use the same table, couch, or chair for going over material for school tests. Dub it the "study corner" and get comfortable.

· ♡ ·

Musical Chairs

Once in a while rotate seating positions at the kitchen or dining room table so children have a turn at the head of the table.

Double Desserts

Once a month or if you happen to have enough, shock your children by announcing double dessert night.

Kid Fix

Request a "kid fix" (a hefty hug and a big kiss) whenever you feel the need and let your child know it makes you feel better.

What a Fine Family This Is!

Flaunt it by placing framed family photographs on tables and walls around the house. Put a group photo in your child's room on his night table or wall.

Not the Teacher's Pet

During rough periods at school, be understanding. Don't be quick to jump on the teacher's bandwagon. Listen to your child's point of view.

Lumpy Vases and Paper Flowers

If your child made it, find a special place for it, not the bottom drawer or the closet shelf. Take his "bowl" to the office to hold paper clips.

Share the Seasons

Point out glorious leaf colors in the fall, a snowcapped mountain in winter. There's a joy in introducing your child to and sharing the natural beauty of the ever changing seasons—or one unusual sight in the landscape.

Diner

"Nothing could be finer than to eat in Mommy's diner." Label your kitchen counter the "diner" and sing the refrain when you serve up short-order meals.

Also Known As

Always put the flowers, a.k.a. weeds, your child picks for you in water.

Shoe Store

Designate a handy chair or step near the door for tying shoelaces. Call it the "shoe store" and invite your child in for lacing.

Caring Questions

How was your spelling test? History test? Did you win the game? Was the Book Fair fun? If you know something important was scheduled that day, remember to ask about it.

Reduce Kid Overload

Eliminate or cut back some of your child's activities so all your free time is not spent shuttling them or waiting for them.

Sharing Secrets

Parent and child can giggle about the secret, enjoy the suspense, and be proud of each other for keeping the secret so long.

Note: Good secrets only—what's for dinner; a gift for another member of the family; holiday plans; a surprise visitor.

Stellar Showing

Make a practice of exhibiting test papers with good grades and/or inspiring teacher comments.

Ties That Bind

Inform your children when relatives send their love or leave a special message. Keep children up-to-date on family news.

Once a Day

Tell your child you love him a minimum of once a day—when you send him off to school, when you tuck him in at night, or anytime in between.

Architect's Delight

Ask for your child's ideas on any home renovation plans, especially if they include his bedroom.

Young Decorator

When sprucing up your child's room, allow her to decide what color (paint, sheets, curtains) theme she prefers. Give choices if you do not want the options limitless (this wallpaper design or that, white or beige walls, for example).

Museum Quality

Find places around the house—hallways, stairwells, bathrooms—to hang or display your child's best art. He will feel very proud of himself and his work if you frame a drawing or painting every few years.

Getting to Know You

Do you know your child's favorite color? Favorite television show? Favorite cartoon character? Favorite game? Book? Sport? When you know his preferences, you know him better.

The Driving Passion

Be interested in what fascinates your child, not what you want or hope will be her passion, so you will be together more often talking about and exploring the things *she* finds intriguing.

Another Dilemma

Don't dismiss a child's problems lightly. Pay attention to what has happened, take the time to hear your child out, and offer concerned, thoughtful advice for finding solutions. Be sympathetic.

Five Minutes More or Less

You can have meaningful exchanges in a minute or two; for some you don't even have to be present. There are so many ways to stay in touch and to solidify your relationship with little things that mean a lot to children.

May I Have This Dance?

After dinner, turn up the radio and dance with your children for a few minutes.

Family Meeting Place

Keep a bulletin board centrally located—in the kitchen, at the bottom of the stairs, near the back door—with a pencil and pad secured to it so family members can jot down their comings and goings and leave messages for each other.

Two Sugars

Ask your child to join you for a cup of coffee or tea. Pour and dilute with sugar and milk according to age.

I'm Concerned

Send a note to the teacher during the first week of school to explain a little bit about your child and to let the teacher know that you want to be involved even though you are a working parent.

Review

Go over—or in the least glance at—your child's school papers as often as you can. Ask to see them if they are not given to you.

Share a Calendar

Enter the family's birthdays, activities, performances, meetings on one calendar. Refer to it together when arranging the day's or week's schedule.

Photosynthesis

Discuss what your child is studying in school be it fossils, word problems, or photosynthesis.

Good Morning

Initiate a wake-up routine: several kisses, a stuffed animal search, two hugs, a double alarm, or sending the dog to jump on your child's bed.

Bugle Call

Be creative. Sing a wake-up song each morning that includes your child's name.

Long Hours

When early departures and late meetings have you missing your children too often, tape-record greetings for them.

Continuous Story

Start a story on the tape recorder. Alternate additions: yours first; your child's next. When you arrive

home late you can look forward to hearing what your offspring added to the story.

A Word a Day

Buy a calendar—A Fact a Day, A Sports Fact a Day, A Word a Day, A Science Fact—and share one page every morning or evening with your children.

Note: Many Fact-a-Day calendars are written specifically for children.

Pretzels, Please

Prepare the grocery list together.

Soup or Salad

Include your child in meal planning. Children have surprisingly good suggestions, if only for the soup, vegetable, or dessert they prefer.

For No Reason

When the whole family is together—especially if that is not very often—give each member the same token surprise. Call it an "S" to heighten the fun. Could be a pair of socks, a flower, stickers, a pad, a pen, a box of crayons, a book.

Stockbrokers in the Making

Choose a stock for each family member to watch

daily in the newspaper. It's exciting for a child to see a stock's progress and to feel part of your grown-up world.

Note: Stocks do not have to be purchased to make tracking one fun and interesting.

Ha, ha!
Tell your child jokes and laugh at his.

Zooming In
Whenever you are taking pictures, hand over the camera. Ask your youngster to take a photograph or two. Using an adult's camera is serious business to a child and the pictures are a reminder of that special privilege.

Photo Gallery
Hang snapshots of special family times—canoeing with a cousin, biking with parents, feeding baby sister— on a mirror or bulletin board in your child's room. Replace dated photos with new ones.

Sing a Song of 25 Cents
Make up songs to go with popular children's songs and nursery rhymes. Original lyrics can be silly whether set to "Row, Row, Row Your Boat" or to your own tunes.

I Like It, Too

At home and in the car listen to your child's favorite songs and sing along with her. In a strong voice, join her for the catchy verses and refrains.

Family Song

Create a song that includes the names of all family members.

What We Have

Occasionally, and as a family, take stock of what you have and be thankful for the ways in which you are fortunate.

· ♡ ·

Where You Stand

Express your opinions. In doing so you share your values and beliefs and let your child know what you think.

Not Fair

Encourage your children to bring complaints about a sibling or an unfair rule to a "round table" for a family discussion. Be open to compromise or suggestions that will rectify the situation.

It's a Sign

Scribble a sign on a shirt cardboard or a large piece of paper to encourage or praise your child—GO as support for an upcoming competition; CONGRATULATIONS for an honor received, a large project completed. It's a sure sign that you care.

Ask the Teacher

Find out if there is anything you can do at home—from helping with long division to packing an extra snack—to improve your child's school performance.

You're Doing Fine

Share your thoughts about school and teacher with your child when you return from an open house or any meetings you have with your child's teachers.

Accentuate the Positive

Go overboard when praising a good report card or school project. Read the teacher's comments with or to your child.

Saved

Saving schoolwork shows you're interested and encourages a child to do better. Mark a cardboard box "Michael—2nd Grade." During the year drop in papers that you wish to save—or all papers to be sorted at a later date.

Keeping Company

Ask your child to keep you company when you fold laundry or wrap presents, when you write notes or are just relaxing. Ask her just to be there, not to help with any of the work.

Act Silly

Chase your child through the house; pretend to be an airplane and soar down on him; do something utterly ridiculous. Be out-and-out silly.

Switching Roles

As an occasional surprise, complete one of your child's regular chores: feed her dog; set the table; make her bed.

In an Emergency

Go over home safety rules and emergency procedures including dialing 911. Be sure your child feels comfortable staying temporarily with a neighbor.

Surprises in the Mail

Use the mail to send a stick of gum, a special pin, a fancy pencil, or other small objects to your child.

Best/Worst

On a regular basis, ask what was the best and worst part of your child's day or week.

Did You Practice?

Five minutes of your undivided attention while your child practices his musical instrument is more encouraging than five hundred pleas to practice.

Duets

Sing while she plays; play while she sings or dances. Joint performance efforts are very supportive and often hilarious.

Applause, Applause

Never be too busy to watch your children's home-made magic or puppet shows and plays. Watch willingly, clap loudly.

So Big

Mark and date an out-of-the-way wall periodically with your child's growth pattern.

Note: Use different color pencils for each child.

Spades, Hearts, Diamonds, Clubs

Teach your child a card trick.

To Save? To Spend?

Discuss what your child plans to save for or spend his allowance on, but don't dictate spending practices. Always give your child his allowance on the same day, without his having to ask for it.

Precious Extra Time

Schedule and floor space permitting, exercise in your child's bedroom to give you more time together.

Just Say No

Ask your child to picture himself saying no to alcohol and other drugs. Have him practice his stand with you.

Lush Plants

Grow a plant together. Stick toothpicks in a sweet potato, the potato in a glass of water, and check it every few days. Or try growing avocado or grapefruit pits.

Whiter than White

Brush your teeth with your child in the morning. It's more fun for young children to have company while they do what they consider a tiresome job.

Closer than Close

Lather up your child's face and give him or her a razor without a blade to shave alongside you. Splash on a few drops of cologne.

Lunch Box Messages

Napkins are a great place for humorous drawings, short notes, or messages of love.

The Everything Sandwich

Stick it in a lunch box or serve it on a weekend—

this combination sandwich, too fat for ordinary mouths, is piled high with a little bit of everything your child loves.

Checking In

Touch base with your child in the middle of the day or right after school to share her latest excitement, which may long be forgotten by the time you get home.

Good-night Call

Call in your good-night kiss and promise an in-person one as soon as you come home.

Just Rewards

Treat your child to an ice cream or frozen yogurt, a cookie or doughnut after a visit to the doctor or dentist.

Noted: I Love You

Leave notes in your child's room, in a schoolbook, or on the kitchen counter for him to find.

At the Library

When you are in the library or the bookstore picking out books for yourself, stop in the children's section and select a few books for your children.

With Love

Inscribe all books you give your children with loving messages and the date.

Little Things from Other Places

Bring home chopsticks or fortune cookies from a Chinese restaurant lunch, a few mints or packet of sugar for a child to use on her morning cereal. Stop for a comic book or a pack of trading cards.

Catching . . . Up

Spend five minutes before dinner tossing a baseball or football now and then. Mark a calendar with a ball or a check to keep track of how well you're catching up.

Thank You

Send your child a blank card filled in with a message of appreciation—"Thank you for helping me rake the leaves," or "Thanks for cleaning up your room," or "Thank you for helping out with your baby brother."

Mail Call

Hold the mail until the entire family is home. Open it together. Give young children the advertisements, catalogs, and bulk mail that you don't read anyway.

Dear Laura

Send your child a quick note or letter once a week or once a month that details what she's been doing or the fun she's been having. Save the letters.

Get Well Soon

Encourage your child to send Get Well cards to friends and relatives or to sign those that you are sending.

Last Licks

Call children to lick the beaters and the bowl whenever you bake.

Share Your PC

Open a file in your computer for your child. Together type in whatever he wishes to create and save: his birthday party guest list, Christmas wish list, letter to a pen pal, a book report.

Puzzle Mania

Before or after dinner each evening, assemble an age-appropriate puzzle together. Keep it on a tray, heavy poster board, or lightweight piece of wood so you can move it if you need the space.

What's Missing?

Ask your children what they would like to do when you have more time together. Put suggestions in a box and pull one out when, in fact, you have the time.

Note: More back rubs, more kisses, more homemade soup, more games, more ball throwing.

Bull's-eye

Hang a dart board in an out-of-the-way corner ready for a round of target practice when you have a few minutes to spare.

Note: Rubber-tipped safety dart sets should be used with young children. Substitute or alternate with a miniature basketball hoop and ball.

How Was Your Day?

Go around the dinner table and have everyone—that means parents, too—tell something about his or her day.

I Vote for the Grand Canyon

Call a family meeting during dinner to discuss vacation plans. Explain options. Let children express their feelings and make suggestions.

Curious George

When dinner conversation goes flat, retitle favorite books and ask for explanations of the new story lines: Curious George Moves In with the Addams Family; Nancy Drew and the Case of Dr Pepper; The Bobbsey Twins Meet the Grateful Dead; The Babysitter Club Runs the Iditarod. Try this with Babar, Ramona, and other familiar characters or titles.

Newsmakers

Discuss a current event once a week or nightly. Select topics of interest to children: record-breaking sales for a toy; an outstanding athletic performance; a medical discovery or ecological advance.

What Should I Wear?

Ask your child to help you select your clothing for the next day (limit the choices to two).

· ♡ ·

Observe

Sit back, relax, and enjoy watching your child involved in an activity.

Snack Time

If you're not going to be home for dinner, schedule a snack break with your child for before you leave or when you return home.

Note: Designate special plates or cups (decorated paper plates are fine) for snack-time use only.

Silly Spelling

When studying for spelling tests, tie each word on your child's list into a fantasy story about him, the family, an upcoming trip, or a special occasion.

I Give!

An abbreviated wrestling match provides physical contact. For the less aggressive, try tickling. And if you don't care for rolling around on the floor, substitute arm wrestling.

Room Visiting

Make a practice of reading a book or the newspaper in your child's room while she is playing, reading, or getting ready for bed.

Sports Fanatics

Discuss yesterday's ball games, matches, and players' stats with your child.

Tub-side

While you have a captive audience, use this time to sing songs and play with younger children, to talk with older children who still want company.

Chit-Chats

Spend a few minutes at bedtime on the end of your child's bed or in a cozy armchair talking. Keep conversations light and noncritical.

> Note: As chit-chats become routine, you or your child will request a chat when one of you has something important to ask or discuss.

Things Grown-ups Don't Do
Start a pillow fight with your child.

Once More
When your child discovers a book he loves, read it again and again if so requested.

Reading Rituals
Remember, older children like to be read to even after they can read themselves. Try one chapter a night.

What's Happening?
Show an interest in what your children are reading by asking them to summarize the plot for you now and again—but not for every book. Anything mandatory is no longer fun.

Remember When?
Children adore stories about a parent's childhood, especially the incidents in which you were embarrassed or did something "stupid."

When You Were Born
Sure attention getters are stories about events leading to your child's birth or what happened on the day she was born.

When You Were Young

Youngsters delight in hearing about their "youth." Five-year-olds love to be told what they did that was smart or funny when they were two or three years old. Tell them about their first words, words they couldn't quite pronounce, the funny way they crawled or climbed.

Grandma's Version

Ask grandparents to tell your children stories about raising you and your childhood.

You Tell Me

Have the children create their own bedtime stories.

Problem Central

Call yourself the "complaint department" and "be open" before final tuck-in so your child can get what, if anything, is bothering him off his chest.

Lullaby and Good Night

Sing the same song or lullaby with your child each night.

Nightly Fanfare

Have a quick bedtime ceremony even if it's only a certain way of puffing the pillow or patting your child's head. Fly a blanket in the air in the elaborate style of a magician before tucking; fold the top sheet a special way.

Fanfare, Continued

In your absence have the baby-sitter follow your nighttime rituals as closely as possible.

Not Home Stories

When you know that you will not be home at bedtime, or if you want to participate in storytime during the day, tape-record a story for the baby-sitter to play.

Anticipation

Talk about plans for the upcoming weekend. Get your child's input.

Nice Note

At bedtime have your child tell you something good that happened that day. It's a positive note to go to sleep on.

Half an Hour,
an Hour or So

The *years a child prefers* to spend time with his parents rather than his friends speed by. If you don't connect now, relating when he is older will be more difficult. Take advantage of all opportunities. Virtually everything you do together brings you closer and has the potential to become a fond memory.

Smooth Start

Eat breakfast with your child. You'll have time to be sure he has his lunch money, books, sneakers, and other necessities for his day. If you're together for breakfast he might not mind your absence at dinner now and then.

I'm Early

Arrive home half an hour or so earlier than usual to push the stroller or to play in the park before dark with your child.

Sand Castles

Climb in the sandbox. Dig and build, too.

Escort

Now and then go into the office late so that you can take your child to school, even if it's only once a month or once every few months.

Getting to Know You

Early on in the school year, take some time to meet all your child's teachers, coaches, even the bus driver, so if you have to call you will have a name and an association when you are discussing your child.

Open House

Attend back-to-school night. Leave a brief note in your child's desk or notebook that tells her how much you enjoyed visiting her classroom and meeting her teacher.

You're Getting Me That!

When your child least expects it, take him to the store and buy something he's been longing to own.

You Were So Adorable

Go through photo albums describing what your children were doing when the pictures were taken. Show *your* childhood pictures and talk about what you did "way back then."

Only the Good Ones

Ask your child to help you select the photos from each roll to go into the family album. Give children the extra photos—those not going into the family album—to start their own picture book.

Homebound Solos

Strengthen a child's sense of individuality by giving her time alone with you at least once a week—talking, reading, cooking, or playing a game—without any siblings.

Beauty Shop

Give your daughter a new hairstyle one evening—a French braid, a few curls, a ponytail in a fancy new holder or one of yours.

Rose Red

Give your daughter a "manicure"; paint her nails the same color as yours.

Up, Down, Side, Step

Although your child may not be able to keep up with you, invite him to join your home exercise program.

Car Wash

A wonderfully messy job from a young child's point of view.

Note: You can always go over the sections your child streaked.

Assistant to the Chef

You'll see more of your child if you enlist his services to fill the bread basket, carry dishes to the table, fill the salt and pepper shakers, or wash the lettuce.

Sup, Sup, Suppertime

Be sure your family eats together unrushed at least

twice a week—or more—with the television off.

Candlelight Dinner

Once every few weeks, put fresh flowers on the table, light dinner candles, and take a moment to express gratitude that you are a family.

Breakfast for Dinner

Unusual enough to be remembered and especially easy when time is short. Serve a dinner of waffles, pancakes, French toast, or another typical morning meal such as scrambled eggs and English muffins.

Tuesday— Ben's Night

Assign each member of the family a night that he is "responsible" for dinner. Everybody helps with the preparation. Even a four-year-old can put hot dogs in a pot before the water boils, tear lettuce leaves for a salad, or pour chocolate sauce on the ice cream.

Junk Food Jaunt

Now and then abandon the kitchen and surprise your child with dinner at her favorite fast-food spot.

What's Cooking?

Cook something with your child at least once a month—pancakes, cookies, muffins. Simple recipes and prepared mixes are good choices for children who usually can't wait to eat whatever they make.

Note: Invest in a children's cookbook to make cooking more interesting for your young chef.

Pizza Party

Buy prepared pizza crust (Italian pizza bread) from your supermarket or *only* the dough from you local pizza parlor. The children punch down the dough and pull it into shape. Have them spread their favorite toppings and the pizza is ready to bake.

On Your Schedule

Bake a batch of cookies for your child's class. Store in your freezer until the time is right to send them in with a note: "Dear Class, Because you studied so hard for the health test." "Because you finished your science projects." Not because it's your child's birthday.

When You're Going Out

If you have evening plans, sit with your children while they eat dinner.

If You Must Do Work

When you have office work to do at home, invite your child to join you in "pretend office" using his coloring books or schoolwork.

Feels like a New Room

Many children like to rearrange the furniture in their rooms. Volunteer to move the bed or the desk to the other wall and listen to their suggestions. Bring home something to brighten up the new arrangement.

Dyno Power

Definition: Imaginary extra strength children get magically when a parent needs help with a job. Call for "dyno power" when you need something retrieved from upstairs, wood for the fire, or the dinner table set. This silly concept somehow overrides the fact that you've asked for help.

Cast Your Ballot

Take your child to the polls with you when you vote.

Walkin' n Talkin'

Go for a brisk family stroll after dinner for exercise and to chat.

Treats

In the middle of a chore or for a homework break, take your child for an unexpected slice of pizza or frozen yogurt.

Behind the Wheel

Use chauffeuring time wisely: Talk with your child instead of listening to the radio (unless you are singing together).

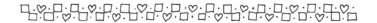

Life after "Go Fish"

As children mature, good card games are I doubt it, crazy eights, hearts, casino, rummy, or gin. Before starting, select a winning score or time limit.

Note: Be flexible; let young children cheat a little, but don't let them win every game.

Game Time

The quickies are: checkers, tic-tac-toe, hangman, backgammon, Uno, and a few rounds of Boggle.

Tournament of Tournaments

Select a game—Monopoly, Clue, Scrabble, Ping-Pong, or pool—play it regularly and keep an ongoing score. Leave game boards set up for the next round.

Note: Cards, too, are excellent for "tournament play."

Foul Shots

Shoot baskets in the local park, schoolyard, or your own driveway.

Relax

You don't always have to be doing something with your children. Your just being home and in the same room is enough.

Checkups

Schedule dental and doctor appointments so that you, not your child's caretaker, can be there for moral support.

Joint Collections

Baseball cards, stamps, coins, board games, bottles, seashells, dollhouse furniture, calendars, salt and pepper shakers. Find a common ground for collecting together.

Showtime

Do whatever it takes to be in the audience for your child's school plays, concerts, and other performances. He'll be looking for you.

Make a Production

Bring flowers to your "star," or take her out to lunch or dinner. Take pictures in costume and post them on the refrigerator or kitchen bulletin board.

Van Gogh in the Making

Even if your skills are nonexistent, sketch or color with your child if you're asked. Amazing conversations and insights come across the calm of the drawing board.

Selective Volunteering

To keep in tune with your child's school life, volunteer for the school fair or carnival booth for an hour or two.

Thank you, Mrs . . .

Make yourself more visible at school without being the class parent. Send each child in your son or daughter's class a tiny pumpkin for the Halloween party—with the teacher's okay, of course.

Note: Offer to supply candy canes or Christmas pencils for the Christmas party.

Another Year Well Done

Celebrate the last day of the school year with a family lunch or dinner in a fancier restaurant than you would normally take the children to. Dress up and make it an occasion.

Weekend Fun

Without plans, weekends slip into drudgery that is chock-full of chores, errands, or pure inertia. Putting forth the extra effort to decide to do something together is what makes a family closer and what makes being one of its younger members more exciting. The suggestions here range from universal to highly specialized. Select ones that suit you and your family's preferences and style.

Time Out

Specify a regular hour or two on Saturday or Sunday or all afternoon on a given weekend to do something special with your children. Activities and outings are big morale boosters.

Over Easy with a Side of Bacon

Go out for breakfast or brunch on a Sunday morning. Let a different member of the family choose the restaurant each time.

Sunday Papers

Read your children's favorite comic strips to them until they can read them to you.

Oven Fresh

Doughnuts, bagels, or blueberry muffins warm from the bakery are a treat the whole family can anticipate. Take the children routinely; let them make the selection.

Initially Yours

Cook pancakes in the shape of your child's initials or make roly-poly people with heads, arms, and legs. Add raisins, blueberries, banana pieces, or chocolate morsels for eyes, noses, mouths, or buttons.

Treat Night

Reserve a weekend evening for popcorn, ice cream, pizza, soda, or another treat not permitted during the week.

What Can We Do?

Keep the house well stocked with board games for rainy days and evenings.

Something New

Learn a new sport together. Take up cross-country skiing, aerobics, or hiking as a family.

Note: This may require some prodding at first.

It's a Blue Jay

Study butterflies, birds, or plant life. Buy appropriate books or borrow them from the library.

A Hole-in-One

Take time out for a round of miniature golf or to drive a bucket of balls.

Do-si-dos

Attend a square dance as a family.

Up, Up, and Away

Try your hand at kite flying.

Needed and Appreciated

Prepare a large pan of lasagna or a batch of stew with your children and deliver it to a local shelter. Call ahead to be sure your gift can be accepted.

Down the River

Locate a river that flows just right for tubing. Check the yellow pages for places that rent large tubes.

Destination Ride

Orchestrate a family bicycle ride that offers an enticing reward—pizza lunch, a swim, a double-dip cone, a visit with someone special.

Note: If you're planning serious biking, state Park Departments issue bicycle route maps.

Family Night

Devote one night—three or four times each year—to skits, charades, board games, or another activity all family members can participate in no matter what their ages.

Don't Burn Mine

Build a fire in the fireplace, find pointed sticks, and roast marshmallows.

Fireside Special

The perfect memory maker: S'mores—roasted marshmallow and sections of chocolate bars sandwiched between two graham crackers. Make them on cold weekend evenings when the family is huddled around the fire.

Fire Fighter

Visit the local fire station with your child.

Cupcakes in the Making

Discover how the filling gets in the middle or ice cream gets its flavors. Find a food factory—bakery or bottling company—in your area that gives tours. The manufacturing process with its automation and assembly lines is impressive and memorable.

Watch It Rise

Measure the ingredients, knead the dough, watch it rise, pound it down, shape it. These are all steps children can help with during an at-home bread making session.

Swinging
String a hammock between two trees and share lazy, restful moments in it together.

No Green Thumb Required
Plant tomatoes—cherry tomatoes do well—in a large clay pot or tub to set out on your deck or apartment balcony during the summer. Have the children water and pick the tomatoes as they ripen.

Green Thumb Required
Start a garden with your children even if you have only a small space. Plant vegetables they like and that produce quickly and in abundance—green beans, peas, tomatoes, zucchini, cucumbers.

So Big
Sunflowers grow as high as ten feet or more. Once grown, they are not forgotten.

So Fat
If you have the space, grow pumpkins from giant pumpkin seeds. Full grown, these special seeds produce pumpkins that can weigh over 450 pounds. Growing normal-size pumpkins is an equally remarkable experience for children.

Red, Yellow, Brown, and Orange

Go for a walk through the leaves and collect the prettiest ones to bring home.

Fall In

Rake together a huge pile of leaves for the children to jump into.

On the Beach

Build very large sand castles with moats and roads.

Note: Car, snake, and turtle shapes are also easy to form in the sand.

Arrowheads and Driftwood

To keep the spirit of a trip alive, make a collection of seashells, rocks, arrowheads, or driftwood. At home, assemble as a collage or keep your collection in a bowl in the family room.

Super Sundaes

Arrange all the fixings—-sprinkles, syrups, fresh fruit—on the kitchen or picnic table and let everyone smother a bowl of ice cream.

A Weekend Dessert

Scoop ice cream into a glass and let each person add chocolate syrup and soda pop to create ice cream sodas that foam and fizz.

The Capital Is

Go to your state capital for the day or weekend.

Tide's Out

When the sandbar is in view, comb the beach for sand dollars. Boil them with bleach to a milky white.

When dry, children have a prize memento.

Matinee Today

Sitting proudly next to Mom or Dad in a darkened theater compensates for long weekday hours at the office.

Monthly Movie

Select "family" movies to attend on Friday or Saturday evenings, Saturday or Sunday afternoons. Invite children to help in the selection.

Down, Boy!

Train or groom your pet together.

Hometown Times

If geographically feasible, make an excursion to the town of your childhood. Point out the movie theater, the basketball court or dance studio, your elementary school—whatever buildings are still standing. Knock on the door of your old home to see if the occupants will show your children through the house.

On Foot

Take a walking tour of your city or town. Libraries and/or the chamber of commerce have listings of the historical sites and points of interest to guide you.

Tents and All

Whether a one-shot or frequent activity, camping out offers opportunity for rich memories.

Camping "In"

Unroll your sleeping bags in the living room and camp in with your children for the night.

For a Good Cause

Whether you're stuffing envelopes for a fund-raiser, pounding signs into the ground for a political campaign, or dropping leaflets about your favorite cause on people's doorsteps, a child volunteer can be as helpful—and certainly as enthusiastic—as his parent.

Good Luck

Hunt for four-leaf clovers together. Press them in a book to save.

Personal Best

Create a walking or jogging loop that starts and ends at your front door and that matches your youngster's age and ability. Return your child to proper supervision, then resume your normal speed and course.

Personal Trainer

If you can be flexible and easygoing about jogging, let your child "pace" you on her bicycle. Most of the time she'll be way ahead and doubling back.

Ferris Wheels and Roller Coasters

Attend the same carnival every year.

The More the Merrier

Join other families to eat and play games right in your own backyard. If everyone brings part of the meal, all you really need to supply is a ball and some bubbles.

Grilled with Frills

Have a cookout for your children's friends. Supply the food and the frills: potato chips, popcorn, and pretzels.

The Oldies

Teach your children how to play hopscotch, marbles, jacks, and pick-up sticks.

Over the River and . . .

Bring the children and the food for a picnic at Grandma's or another relative's home.

Change of Pace

Party food on paper plates by the fireplace constitutes a fine midwinter indoor picnic.

Regulars

Make grandparents, an aunt, or another relative a regular diner at your table for a family meal during the weekend.

No Excuses

Plan one weekend evening for the family to stay home and do something together—watch a video, cook, put a room in order, sort the audio collection. Accept no excuses for missing this time together.

Surprise Guest

Invite a surprise person—an old family friend, a relative, one of your child's friends—to dinner and keep it a secret until he or she walks in the door.

You're Invited

Include one of your child's favorite coaches, instructors, or special teachers in a family event or invite him or her to join you for a taco or spaghetti dinner.

Our Night Out

Select a night to go to a ball game or bowling or to

some event, just Dad and children. It's a night to consume as many soft drinks as your child wants.

Dress Up
While you're dressing for an evening out, your daughter can be donning clothing you've discarded but saved in a box or bag (on the floor of your closet) for these occasions.

You Never Know What You'll Find
Spend a few hours scouting flea markets or garage sales. Given a minimal amount of money, a child can unearth what he believes is a treasure—which it may well be one day.

What a Funny Gerbil
Visit the pet store periodically.

Family Doubles
Pair up for tennis as soon as your children can hold rackets. They'll like being on the court even if they can't hit the ball over the net. In a few years family tennis will be fun for parents, too.

Superb Craftsmanship
Plan an ongoing project. Build a model airplane, boat, or car with your child and keep it displayed on

a shelf no matter how it turns out.

Pickings That Are Not Slim

Schedule an afternoon of strawberry, blueberry, raspberry, or apple picking. Harvest dates and locations are listed in local newspapers.

Jam Session

Children can help gather and prepare the fruit, add the necessary ingredients, and stir the pot. Even failed (runny) jam or jelly is a delicious replacement for chocolate syrup over ice cream.

Bumper Bowling

Call your bowling alley to see if they offer "bumper bowling." With the gutters blocked with air-filled tubes, bowling can be a no-miss proposition even for the youngest bowlers.

Please Touch

Choose a hands-on museum over a regular viewing musuem for children. Interactive museums are stimulating and more enjoyable for the young set.

True Soul Mates

Amaze your child with a stop to play video games together in the nearest arcade.

The Big Bite

Drop a fishing line from a bridge or cast it from the edge of a creek. Many municipalities stock their lakes and streams, and sporting goods stores often rent poles.

Note: Find out if you need a fishing permit, what's the best lure and bait for catching local fish. And bring your camera.

Not Bored

Car trips are enjoyable excursions when children are occupied. Take along hand-held games, age-appropriate travel toys, a small pillow and a blanket for each child.

Imagine If

What would you do if you were mayor of your city? Principal of your school? Owner of a baseball team? Conductor of an orchestra? Ask your child as you drive to your destination.

Chores That Bond

Certain jobs when tackled as a team can be fun and breed a warm brand of togetherness: raking leaves, planting a garden, and straightening out toy chests.

Note: The jobs children complain about the loudest are the ones most often remembered with fondness.

Permanent Structures

Work with your child when creating a stone wall, building a walkway, or making lasting changes to your property.

Fisher & Company

Join with your son or daughter to fix a pipe, clear a

gutter, or wash the windows. Your child's sense of accomplishment is enhanced when you joke about the fact that it was "another job well done by (Your Last Name) and Company."

· ♡ ·

Party Time

Make a big deal out of shopping for party and special-occasion attire for your children.

Just Like Mom's/Dad's

When clothes shopping for special family events, such as weddings or Christmas, buy gloves or a bracelet, something that matches Mom's; a shirt or jacket that resembles Dad's; or color-coordinate the whole family.

Mother/Daughter–Father/Son Annual Spree

Focus attention on your child by making a day of back-to-school shopping even if she only needs shoes and a notebook. Go to lunch afterwards.

Role Models

Bring the children to local high school sporting events, concerts, and plays. Seeing other youngsters perform is inspiring.

Victory Dinner

Celebrate your team with a casual restaurant dinner or ice cream after a victory.

The Perfect Excuse

Use Derby Day or Super Bowl Sunday as an excuse to invite friends and their children over to watch the event and to share sandwiches or pizza.

Major Decisions

Have the children plan the evening—where to eat and what the after-dinner activity will be.

Bingo!

Schedule a weekend afternoon or evening of bingo. Cover the numbers and encourage the children to shout "Bingo!" Hand out small prizes to add to the excitement.

Super Hero

Buy the longest Italian breads you can find and lots of sandwich fixings. Let each person add a layer, then cut your bulging super hero into sections.

> *Note: Alternate preparation—divide bread first, let everyone prepare his own.*

The Collector

Help your young collector—of stamps, coins, base-ball cards, comic books—by attending a special show or visiting a store to add more items to his accumulation. When traveling, remember to buy a collected item as a souvenir.

Special Events

Plan a unique outing—not necessarily costly—in advance. Mark it on the calendar and talk about it to build up enthusiasm.

> *Note: A few possibilities are kayaking, cross-country skiing, attending children's theater or puppet shows.*

Batter Up

Find other families and arrange to play ball together. Be sure you have enough players for two teams.

Space Permitting

Set up a volleyball net or croquet set in your yard. Or hang a basketball hoop from the garage.

Travel Time

Take a trip. Trips encourage family unity and feed the memory bank.

We Were There

Send your child a postcard from places you visit together—even for the day or a few hours. "We had a great time, didn't we? Loved being with you."

After the Fact

Whatever you do, relive the experiences to ingrain them in your child's memory. Discuss the event, its mishaps, coincidences, and humorous turns.

· ♡ ·

Missing You

Tell your children when you feel unhappy about being away from home so much.

Big Bed

Now and then allow your child to sleep in your bed as an extra privilege while you are away.

Soft and Fluffy

Give your child your pillow to sleep with whenever you're traveling.

Oversized

One of Dad's or Mom's T-shirts is the perfect child's nightshirt when you're out of town.

The Unexpected

Leave short notes in surprise places for your child to discover.

A Note a Day

Ask questions or comment on an event scheduled for each day you will be away. Put your thoughts in writing in separate envelopes marked Monday, Tuesday, Wednesday . . . Have the baby-sitter or other parent deliver the appropriate envelope each day.

Privileges

Put special "rules" into effect when you're traveling—add a few extra minutes to bedtime, an extra television program, a favorite meal twice.

Dinner Guest

While you're away, allow your child to have a friend stay for dinner even though it may be a school night.

City by City

Instead of purchasing useless junk, buy a mug with a city logo or sports team emblem from each city you visit on business. Mugs will be used for years by the recipient and/or the entire family.

Note: Caps/hats, magnets, and city spoons make interesting collections, too.

Prized Possession

The free pad of paper, pen, or shampoo in your hotel room which is meaningless to you, often becomes a child's prized possession. Bring it home.

Today Was Rainy

Mail postcards home every day or two. Explain something about the city, a special building, landmark, or historical sight. Write about an unusual

meal, mode of transportation, or funny incident to make your child feel a part of your trip.

Welcome Home

Plan a simple welcome home celebration in honor of your return: a favorite meal, treat, or activity to do together.

Flight #272

Have your spouse and children meet you for the weekend at the end of a business trip. Hotels offer low weekend rates and special weekend family packages.

Business Pal

Bring your child to conventions whenever possible. Business trips with lengthy flights and long, lonely evenings are opportunities to spend extended time with your children.

Note: During the day many of the major hotels offer child care and supervised activities.

Room Service

It's cozy and an exceptional treat for children. Allow yours to do the ordering.

SICK DAYS

T_he kindnesses displayed_ by a parent or caregiver for a child who is ill are expressions of love. Warm memories develop from the extra effort or "royal" treatment while your child is recovering.

In Sickness and in Health

Being apart from your child is a fact of life, so try not to feel guilty. Make the best care arrangements you can.

Long Stem

Bring home a single rose or a small bunch of flowers for the patient's room.

Believing

Acknowledge that your child doesn't feel well if she says so. Ask what is wrong and offer suggestions that may make her feel better.

Don't Panic

Do not overreact or keep asking your child how he feels. By staying calm you let him know that you are in control and he can feel safe in your care.

Fancy, Fancy

An attractive tray makes the food more appetizing. Use a bright-colored napkin, fancy dishes, Dad or Mom's coffee mug for soup or juice.

What Service!

As a special treat, bring your patient her food in bed even if she is well enough to come to the table.

It's All in the Presentation

Prepare foods differently for the bed- or couch-ridden patient: Cut toast into triangles or small squares; put ice cream in a glass instead of a bowl; make a milk shake; serve sodas and juices with a straw.

Nurse Jones

Refer to yourself as the nurse and take temperature or dispense medicine with hospital-like fanfare. Be humorous.

Explanations Help

Be sure your child understands how his medicine works or how liquids aid the body's healing. Explain as best you can what will happen during a doctor's visit or hospital stay.

· ♡ ·

Choices

The ill child will feel more in control if allowed to have choices whenever possible: a bath or a sponge bath, a game of Sorry or Clue, fruit juice or soda, an ice pop or ice chips, and so forth.

Couch Potato

Let your patient spend the day on the couch or in your bed.

TLC
Wash the patient, give her clean pajamas and a hair comb—a new style if she's up to it—and puff the pillows before returning her to bed.

Roll Up the Sleeves
Offer your child Dad's pajamas or Mom's sleep shirt.

Calling All Parents
Give the bedridden child a bell to ring or a whistle to blow when he needs you.

At Her Fingertips
Set up a table or use an existing nightstand to have everything the patient needs in easy reach—water, tissues, crayons, books.

In Reserve
Have a few brand-new activity books hidden in a closet to give to a sick child before you go to work.

The Royal Treatment
Sick days are the time to disburse as much special treatment as time permits. As your child's health improves, color with him, play cards, read him a book, or sit quietly in his room when you are home.

It's Lunch Time

If you work nearby, stop home during your lunch break to say hello or to share a tray meal with your homebound child.

A Fresh Look

Supply a different blanket, different sheets, or a pillowcase not normally used by the children.

Be Patient

Don't send your child back to school before he is ready.

How Are You Feeling?

Call home from the office a few times a day to check on your sick child, to speak with her and to reassure yourself.

Bedridden and Bored

Break up the monotony with a hat and a deck of cards. Place the hat on the foot of the bed and see how many cards your child can toss into it.

Early Arrival

The day is long for a sick child. Come home as early as possible to be with him.

Extra Attention

When you are home during a child's recuperation, check on her frequently; deliver extra kisses and hugs.

Magic Hour

Give your child something to look forward to: Set a specific hour—late afternoon, before or after dinner—that you will play a game with him or stay with him.

Bedtime Busywork

Promise to bring home a surprise—a comic book, a coloring book, a new set of markers or crayons, a puzzle book, a reading book, a model.

I Need You

Be sure the sick child knows that she can call you during the night, that you will be there if she needs you.

The Doctor Will See You

Bring a book to read or a quiet game to play together in the doctor's waiting room.

On the Mend
Put Mom's favorite bubble bath in the bathwater.

Another's Illness
When a child learns of a friend's injury or illness, take the time to explain and answer his questions. Invariably, young children worry that the same fate will befall them.

Special Days
HAPPY HOLIDAYS

Whatever you celebrate, include ritual, start or continue traditions. Repetition of happy celebrations fuels feelings of closeness. Every holiday—be it George Washington's Birthday or Christmas—offers fertile ground for creating positive and strong family unity.

Wrap It Up

Hold sessions for children to wrap—or help wrap—gifts they are giving. To speed things along and make it more fun, set up a "wrapping station" on a counter or table with paper, scissors, tape, ribbons, and stickers from which children can pick what they like.

Holiday Staple

Include at least one preferred dish or dessert at every holiday meal each year—an unusual stuffing for the turkey, sweet potatoes with marshmallows, a pecan pie that your great-grandmother made, or a new recipe that everyone loved last year and is fast becoming the family's first choice.

The Good Old Days

Family gatherings are ideal for videotaping senior members. Ask each older relative to relate a family tale. By videotaping at holiday celebrations you will accumulate a wonderful family history for your children to treasure.

Wishing

Save and dry the wishbones from holiday turkeys or chickens for the children to break a few days later. When the leftovers are gone, the wishbone extends holiday spirit a bit longer.

Gobble, Gobble

Heighten the delight by placing a small chocolate turkey at each child's table setting.

Pumpkin Pie—Yuk!

Traditional Thanksgiving pies often don't appeal to the young set. Augment the dessert offerings by buying or baking some more suited to children's taste: seven-layer cake, brownies, or cupcakes.

Cooking Specialist

Ask for cooking help. Turn one child into a stuffing mixer; another into a potato masher, pie dough roller, or ingredient chef. Assign the same tasks each Thanksgiving; children quickly become both proud and protective of their "product."

· ♡ ·

All Together Now

Unless the children make a special request, don't isolate them at a separate table in another room. Bring the kitchen table into the living room or rent a larger table so that everyone can enjoy the holiday meal together.

Put Aunt Lynda next to Uncle Gordon

Let the children arrange the seating for holiday

dinners. Purchase plain white cards in a stationery store and have the children add a turkey or other appropriate sticker.

Note: Since many of the same people attend holiday meals, you can save the place cards for next year.

Spilling Is Allowed

Eliminate holiday intimidation and endear yourself to children and guests by making a predinner announcement not to worry about spills and mishaps.

Note: Save your best tablecloths for formal dining, not for holiday meals with children.

Walk It Off

Gather the entire clan and go for a long walk after Thanksgiving dinner or between the main course and dessert.

The Menorah, the Tree

Shop as a family for special holiday items and decorations such as the menorah for Hanukkah or the Christmas tree.

Chose It Myself

Take each child shopping individually for gifts for her siblings and for your spouse.

A Caring Christmas

With the children, search closets and chests for coats, clothing, toys, and canned foods to give to the homeless and needy.

Special Delivery

Take your children when you deliver gifts to hospitalized children or social service groups.

Holiday Bake-In

Way in advance, before you're feeling stressed by other holiday preparations, select cookie recipes children can decorate. Bake and store in your freezer.

· ♡ ·

"A" is for Andrew

Use the tail end of the cookie batter to shape your child's initial into a cookie he decorates.

Gingerbread House

Build and decorate it together. An impressive and splendid effort that's worth the time in the memory department.

Town Tour

Ride or walk around the neighborhood one evening to see the Christmas lights.

'Twas the Week Before Christmas

Excitement levels are soaring and children need more of your time and direction to keep them calm and occupied. Try to get home earlier to accomplish much of the busywork of Christmas and to spend more time preparing with your children.

On Display

Select a bowl or basket, the mantel or door frame for showing the Christmas cards you receive. Use the same "holder" every year so it becomes part of your Christmas tradition.

Extra Kisses

Hang mistletoe in heavily trafficked areas of the house: over the refrigerator door, the back door, the bathroom, or your child's bedroom door.

Time Out

Find five minutes during each hectic holiday to have private time with your child. Offer her the opportunity to allow her to complain, relax, or just sit quietly close to you.

Come in from the Cold

Keep plenty of marshmallows and cocoa on hand to make hot chocolate after outdoor activities.

Frosty

Be willing to get cold and wet when making a snowman, sledding, or ice skating with your child.

Tree Tradition Options

Go into the woods and cut down your Christmas tree every year. Or buy rooted trees and plant them after Christmas to watch them grow for years to come.

The Angel Goes on the Top

Choose tree decorating time carefully—when children are not tired and adults are not preoccupied. Plan it as a family event.

New Additions

Give your child a new tree ornament each Christmas. If you have time and the inclination, there are kits for making decorations . . . with your child, of course.

"This Is My Favorite"

As you decorate, reminisce with your child about the ornaments—where they came from, stories behind them. Use and save the shaggiest of school- and homemade ornaments.

The Stockings Were Hung

Your child's stocking is for a lifetime. Whether you buy, knit, needlepoint, or have someone else make it, be sure this very special part of Christmas is high quality.

Dear Santa

Before going to sleep, have your child write a note to Santa—or write it for him—and leave it next to some cookies and milk (perhaps a carrot for the reindeer). In disguised handwriting, leave Santa's response.

Who Filled It?

In large families with older children, pull names out of a hat to see who will fill which family member's stocking. Keep names secret until Christmas morning; set a cost limit on stocking stuffers.

Young Santas

To help instill the spirit of giving, have the children pass out the presents one at a time.

Where Is It?

Hide one gift for each child to find.

I Can't Wait

If your tradition is to open gifts on Christmas morning, have each person open one gift Christmas Eve; if your tradition is to open gifts Christmas Eve, save one per person for Christmas morning.

The High Sign
Agree on a signal that alerts you when your child wants to talk to you alone, away from the commotion.

A Family Tale
Create a fun or fantasy story about your family—its members near and far, achievements, and goals—to read as part of one evening's festivities. Ask each member for his thoughts and write down his contribution to the tale.

Strawberry Pancakes
Establish a traditional Christmas morning breakfast in your house—a special kind of pancakes, sticky buns, fancy omelets, or jelly-filled crepes.

Windows
Avoid the crowds viewing the store windows in your city's shopping area by going the day after Christmas. After all, Christmas is a season, not a day. Stop for hot chocolate.

The Nutcracker
Attend high school holiday plays, which are almost

always appropriate for young children. Save the longer, professional productions for when the children are older.

Dress Up

Put on festive clothing for holiday dinners, outings, and get-togethers.

Tradition

Serve one or more of the traditional dishes during Hanukkah.

Eight Nights

Be consistent about handing out Hanukkah gifts. Determine whether gift time will be after lighting the candles or at the conclusion of dinner.

Toast Master

Allow each child to make a toast or offer thanks for a holiday meal. As children get older, alternate speakers from year to year.

Salute

Reserve extra minutes before you go off to your own party to deliver Happy New Year cheer to your children. Serve a special snack and soft drinks in fancy glasses for toasting.

At the Stroke of Midnight

Include your children in the New Year celebration by leaving them party hats and noisemakers and by calling home just before their bedtimes.

At-Home New Year's Eve

Make your New Year's Eve or New Year's Day menu as traditional as the one you plan for Christmas so that the family will have another festivity to look forward to.

Happy New Year

Give each child a small New Year's gift.

Waiting for Midnight

On Christmas give the children a board game with the express intention of playing it as part of a family New Year's Eve celebration.

Little Holidays, Big Deal

Make a big deal out of the small holidays. Drop green food coloring into the mash potatoes or a batch of cookie dough for St. Patrick's Day; bring home a cherry pie for George Washington's Birthday; buy candy apples for Halloween.

Instant Holiday

Turn any holiday meal into a festive celebration by purchasing theme-decorated paper napkins and/or plates—with shamrocks for St. Patty's Day, hearts for Valentine's Day, flags for July Fourth, pumpkins for Halloween, bunnies for Easter.

Fat Tuesday

For Mardi Gras, the last night before Lent, make a pancake dinner. The traditional purpose was to use up all the fat in the house.

Food for Fun

On Halloween Eve or Halloween night, serve only foods in the holiday colors. Some orange and black menu choices: hamburgers on pumpernickel bread; carrots, yams, olives, "blue" corn tortilla chips, orange soda or juice, orange slices, devil's food cake, or cupcakes with orange frosting.

Happy, Sad, or Scary

Set aside a half hour after dinner to carve or paint faces on one large family pumpkin or several small ones every year. Choose Halloween pumpkins as a family.

In the Halloween Spirit

Dress a scarecrow and hang decorations every Halloween.

Ghosts and Goblins

Stop in the bakery for cookies shaped as witches, pumpkins, ghosts, or goblins and covered with thick orange and black icing.

Trick or Treat
Keep your child company as she goes from door to door.

In Costume
Give trick-or-treaters and your child a thrill by appearing in costume or by donning a mask, a baseball cap, or a strange combination of clothing just to answer the doorbell and pass out treats.

Annual Loot Survey
Have your child pour his treats on the table for you to make a safety check and to select several pieces of your favorite candy. After a few Halloweens your child will make a ritual of handing over pieces of the candy you like best.

Daily Sweet
Store extra Halloween candy in a container in the freezer to pack in lunches or for snacks. Send your child to the freezer to pick a treat for the day.

Be Mine
Remember your child on Valentine's Day with a card, candy, and/or a small gift.

Kisses, Kisses Everywhere

Leave a trail of chocolate kisses for your child to follow. Place a few kisses in his cereal bowl on Valentine's Day morning.

All Heart

Buy heart-shaped baking pans—you'll use them every year—and bake a Valentine's Day cake. Use red food coloring to turn the icing pink.

Valentine Lunch

Cut bread into hearts to make a Valentine sandwich or Valentine French toast for breakfast or weekend brunch.

The Color Red

Buy or make cupcakes with pink icing, a strawberry pie, or serve thawed strawberries or raspberries over ice cream. In short, red says "I Love You" on Valentine's Day.

Say "Cheese"

Every Mother's and/or Father's Day, have someone take a few family photos. Save the best shot from each year. As they accumulate, put four or five of them together in an album or frame. It's a colorful record of the passing years.

Major Fun, Major Mess

Standing about a foot apart at first, have two children toss a *raw* egg back and forth. Increase the distance after each successful catch. An outdoors-only Easter event.

Egg Hunt I

Local hotels and inns often plan Easter egg hunts. Join in, then stay for brunch.

Egg Hunt II

Make the hunt a neighborhood happening with each family contributing a predetermined number of colored eggs.

Easy Find

Instead of leaving the Easter basket in plain sight, hide it. Say "Warmer; colder" as your child gets closer to or farther away from the hiding spot.

A Tisket, a Tasket

Each year use the same basket. You can update its look by changing the color ribbons, "straw," and what you put in it.

The Healthy Basket

Filled with a few inexpensive gifts, healthy snacks,

and colorful eggs, a nutritious Easter basket will be as coveted as one laced with too much candy.

July Fourth
Take the children to the local parade and/or fireworks display every year.

Old Glory
To recognize Independence Day, hang a large flag or fly a small one for each child.

Red, White, and Blue
Dress the children in patriotic colors. Wear them yourself.

The Winner Is . . .
Hand out red, white, and blue crepe paper and streamers to neighborhood children for a bicycle decorating contest. Hold a bicycle parade for parent "judges."

Get Together
Plan a family, friends, or neighborhood July Fourth celebration picnic.

MEMORABLE BIRTHDAYS

Birthdays, like holidays, are naturals for building tradition. Your child's birthday is a celebration that he or she is part of your life. Make it more than just another day with a cake. If you don't make birthdays special, your child may not feel special.

Queen/King for a Day

Purchase a fancy crown in a party or toy store to be worn by the birthday child each year.

Birthday Wake-Up

Place a blown up balloon on the juice glass, a birthday napkin next to the cereal bowl, or hang a Happy Birthday sign for a wake-up surprise.

It's Your Birthday

Ask your child what kind of cake, what kind of party (define limits), and what friends she would like on her birthday. Being part of the planning enriches the day.

Gray-Brown Icing

The birthday cake holds more appeal for children if they had a hand in making and decorating it. Whether from scratch or a mix, start a custom of preparing each family member's birthday cake together.

Place of Honor

Seat the celebrant at the head of the dinner table. Let him choose the birthday meal.

Growing, Growing, Growing

Mark a height chart on each birthday.

Early Risers
Leave a gift on the foot of your child's bed so he wakes up to a present.

All-Day Surprises
Scatter gifts throughout the day—put one in her backpack; one in the lunch box; leave one on the kitchen table for after school.

Hidden Treasures
Hide gifts in one or two rooms around the house.

Flying Balloons
Hang a balloon from the mailbox, a tree, or the doorknob to welcome the birthday child home from school.

Designer Cakes
Make an unusual cake in a special shape—a car, a dinosaur, a teddy bear, an airplane, a football—and decorate it accordingly or match the cake design to the party theme.

Instant Decorating
Decorate simply. Some balloons, a few colorful streamers, and birthday napkins do the trick.

Traditional Signs

Buy or design Happy Birthday messages to hang year after year. Or write on a piece of cardboard in marker, The Big 1-0, Happy 6th . . .

Blindfolded and Swinging

Hang a different type of piñata every year.

Can We Play?

Repeat preferred party games every year.

Memorable Memorabilia

Save birthday cards, unusual bows, cake or room decorations. Also stow away a copy of the party invitation and a birthday napkin from each party.

Photocopy Invitations

Turn a child's drawing into a party invitation by writing the party information below the picture and photocopying the number you need.

Do-It-Yourself Cloth

Spread a plain (heavy-weight) white paper cloth or put sheets of drawing paper at each place with an individual box or group of crayons. Ask each guest to decorate her own place at the party table.

Day with Dad or Mom

Have your child plan a day alone with you: a train ride, boat ride, trip to a department store, picnic in the park or at the zoo. This is especially memorable if you are often away from your child.

Private Birthday

Select a day close to your child's birthday for a private lunch or dinner celebration—just the two of you.

The Art of Giving

Take other members of the family shopping for birthday gifts for the celebrant.

Record the Year

Write a letter to your child each year on his birthday. For younger children, note milestones and progress; for older children praise accomplishments or include the year's special events.

One to Grow On

Plant a birthday tree or shrub in the yard and watch it grow up with your child. Hemlock, white pine, and maple trees grow quickly, so you will be able to see progress from year to year.

Little Things Long Remembered

Childhood *is an adventure* to be joined by parents whenever possible. By grabbing pockets of time together—a few minutes here and there—you create pleasant memories for both you and your child.

In these short intervals you give a child a clear sense of attachment to your family unit. The "little things" offered here help develop that sense of belonging.

Famous Firsts

Be on hand for every first you can initiate: first bus ride, first trip to the dentist, first day of school, first friend's birthday party, first movie in a theater.

Reading, 'Riting, and 'Rithmetic

Record on film the excitement of your child dressed and ready for the first day of school each year.

For Posterity I

Take pictures at all family and school functions.

For Posterity II

Videotape significant happenings from first words and steps to Little League games and birthdays.

Wish I Could Be There

Ask a friend, another parent, or even an older child to videotape a sporting event, recital, or special activity that you cannot attend. View the video with your child.

Getting to Know Me

Take your child to your place of employment for a short visit. If you work in a facility that children cannot visit, ask a co-worker to take photographs of you "in action."

Office Outing

Whenever possible, suggest an office picnic or special outing that includes children so yours can meet your associates.

Remembrances of Things Past

Take pictures of your child's room every few years so she will be able to recall it as it was. Also photograph the exterior of your home(s) and your child's school(s).

Lunch Break

If you work near your child's school and children are permitted to leave the building, take your child out to lunch every once in a while.

Just Moved

Acquaint yourself and your child with your new neighborhood. Make an adventure of locating the library, stores, parks, school, restaurants, the police and fire stations.

New Home

Have a celebration on the first night in a new house or apartment. Toast with soda or milk and cookies; make a gigantic bowl of popcorn to eat while you unpack.

Note: Before you leave your old home and neighborhood, take lots of photographs.

A Friend in Need

Be sure your child has a buddy in his new school. Check this with his teacher very early in the year by note or telephone or at the first parent/teacher conference.

Star Salesperson

When your child is selling cookies for the Girl Scouts, candy for her soccer team, magazines for her school, or wrapping paper for another group, bring the fund-raising order sheet to the office and be her sales force.

Fantasy

For car trips, waiting rooms, or when there is nothing to do, make up stories about people you don't really know. The policeman you just passed lives in a huge castle; the nurse in the doctor's office is a ballet dancer at night. Ask your child to develop the stories.

Helping the Homeless

As a family save pennies—or nickels, dimes, and quarters—in a jar. Once counted, deliver the money to an agency that serves the homeless in your area.

It Adds Up
Save, count, and roll change with your child.

Open a Bank Account
Go to the bank together to fill out the forms and obtain a passbook.

Red Envelopes
Instead of just handing over gift money or allowance, put it in colored envelopes. The envelope quickly becomes a welcome and unique family custom.

My Stuff
Purchase a bath towel, a rocking chair, a mug—any item that is used often—with your child's name on it.

Dream House
Over time—years, in fact—decorate a dollhouse with your child.

Happy Un-birthday to You
Chose a day roughly six months from a child's real birthday and deem it his un-birthday. Give the day a quirky name, such as Zebra Day, Muffin Day, or Me, Myself, and I Day, and let him choose what he would like to wear, to do, and to eat.

The Sixties Revisited

Sing songs from decades gone by. Your children will think your performance is perfectly awful. They'll complain, but they'll remember your singing affectionately.

Tall Tales

Save your family's "made-up" stories—especially ones in which the children are the central characters—on paper or a computer disk for them to reread.

Awards Ceremony

At the last dinner or lunch of a vacation, present awards to each of the children. Awards need not be fancy: an empty box of cereal to the best eater, a tennis ball to the most enthusiastic sportsman, a used paperback to the person who read the most, candy to the most congenial, a comic book to the funniest. Make up awards to fit whatever activities you've enjoyed.

T-shirt Quilt

Store your child's outgrown souvenir T-shirts, those collected from vacations, received as gifts, and brought home from your business trips, to turn into a quilt.

> *Note: Making the quilt can be an ongoing family project or one for your retirement years.*

Can We Go Back?

When you find a vacation spot the whole family enjoys, return on a regular basis for repeat visits.

Voting Power

Plan vacations as a family. As children get older, give them more say in the decision.

No Extra Vacation Days

Can't get enough time off? Send your child to visit a special friend or on a trip with a grandparent. Reciprocate visits with out-of-town friends.

Cuddle Up

It may take you some time, but knit or crochet a scarf, sweater, or, for the very ambitious, an afghan. One homemade item—even mittens or a hat—makes a lasting, loving impression on a child.

Pen Pal

Set your child up with a pen pal from another country and help her keep the correspondence going.

Jack Jones

Have pencils and stationery imprinted with your child's name.

Back to Nature
Try to keep the animals—box turtles, lizards, crickets—long enough to emblazon their discovery on your child's mind before releasing them to their natural environment.

Monthly
Order subscriptions to magazines that interest your child at different stages and through different phases.

On My Own
The first few times your child goes away with another family or to spend time with relatives, slip a note into his suitcase to remind him that you love him and are thinking about him.

On Arrival
Mail a letter or postcard ahead so it's waiting for your child when she arrives for her first day of camp each year.

Keepsakes
Find a sturdy box, a plastic or metal storage container, or a durable folder to store programs, buttons, ticket stubs, and other "treasures" from events your child attends.

Surprise Packages
Now and again send home whatever you've bought for your son or daughter. Have the store ship the package addressed to your child.

Treasure-trove
Save your child's class photographs and report cards together in one safe place.

From the Library Of
Favorite books should be put aside for you and your child to reminisce about or for him to give to his own children years from now.

My Teddy
Carefully wrap and tuck away your youngster's favorite teddy bear, stuffed animal, or doll when she has outgrown it.

Portraits
Every few years have a professional photographer take pictures of your child.

Capture an Age
Consider having an artist paint an oil or watercolor portrait of your child.

We Want a Dog
Bring home a turtle or a few goldfish.

Little Things Long Remembered
Bring home a kitten or a puppy.